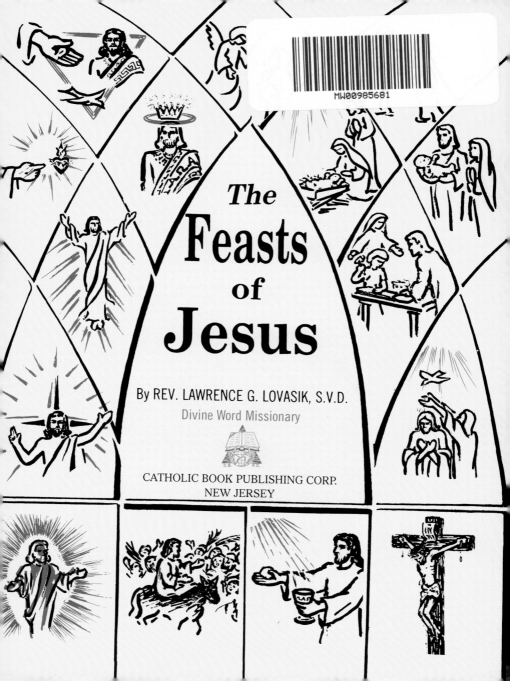

The
Feasts
of
Jesus

By REV. LAWRENCE G. LOVASIK, S.V.D.

Divine Word Missionary

CATHOLIC BOOK PUBLISHING CORP.
NEW JERSEY

THE ANNUNCIATION

The STORY of this Feast . . .

THE angel Gabriel was sent from God to Nazareth and said to the Virgin Mary: "Hail, full of grace! The Lord is with you. Blessed are you among women."

Mary wondered what this greeting meant. But the angel told her: "Do not fear, Mary. You have found favor with God. You will be the mother of a Son and give him the Name Jesus.

2

© 1981 by Catholic Book Publishing Corp., N.Y. - ISBN 978-0-89942-301-2 Printed in Hong Kong

He will be called the Son of God. He will be a King forever."

The angel then said: "The Holy Spirit will come upon you. Your Son will be the Son of God."

Mary said: "I am the servant of the Lord. Let it be done for me as you say." Then the angel left her.

The MEANING of this Feast . . .

GOD invited Mary to become the Mother of His Son. When Mary said "yes," the Divine Word, the Second Person of the Holy Trinity, became a child in His Mother Mary. In nine months He was to be born.

Mary is the Mother of God because she is the Mother of the Son of God. Her prayers to her Son are most powerful.

The Annunciation of the Lord is celebrated on March 25.

THE VISITATION

The STORY of this Feast . . .

MARY went as quickly as she could to visit her cousin, Elizabeth, who was to have a child in her old age. When Mary arrived, Elizabeth cried out: "Blessed are you among women and blessed is the Child of your womb.

"Who am I that the Mother of my Lord should come to me? You are blessed for believing the word of God."

And Mary said: "I am filled with love and praise for God. Though I am only a poor girl, He has given me the greatest of honors. Till the end of time the whole world will call me blessed, for God has done great things for me. His name is holy. He is merciful to those who love and honor Him."

Mary and Elizabeth were very happy. Mary was to give birth to the Son of God, and Elizabeth was to be the mother of John the Baptist who would prepare the way for Jesus. Mary stayed with her cousin three months.

The MEANING of this Feast . . .

JESUS wishes to show us that he gives us His graces through the prayers of His Mother. But all graces come from Him.

The feast of the Visitation is celebrated on May 31.

CHRISTMAS

The STORY of this Feast . . .

JOSEPH and Mary had to travel to Bethlehem to be taxed because Joseph came from the family of King David, who was born in this town.

No one had room for Mary and Joseph, so they had to go to a stable. That night Mary gave birth to her Child. The Savior of the world was born. God had sent His own Son into the world. Mary wrapped Him in soft cloths. She put some hay in the manger out of which the animals ate. Mary laid the Baby Jesus on the hay.

The MEANING of this Feast . . .

GOD loved us so much that He sent His only Son to save us. Jesus became a Man to make us children of God. He gives us the very life of God and the power to be happy forever with God in heaven.

Christmas is celebrated on December 25.

PRESENTATION OF JESUS
IN THE TEMPLE

The STORY of this Feast . . .

IT was a custom among the Jews that when a baby boy was a month old he was brought to the Temple and given to the Lord. So Mary and Joseph brought Jesus to Jerusalem.

A good old man named Simeon was led by the Spirit of God to the Temple. He took Jesus into his arms and praised God. "Now, Lord, I am ready to die, for I have seen the promised Child Who is to be the Savior of the world."

Simeon then said to Mary: "Because of your Child, many in Israel will fall and rise, for He will not be received by all. A sword will pierce your own soul."

The MEANING of this Feast . . .

WHEN only forty days old, Jesus was offering Himself to His heavenly Father as a sacrifice for the salvation of the world in the arms of His Mother.

She now offered her Son to God as she would offer Him standing beneath the cross on Calvary.

The feast of the Presentation of the Lord is celebrated on February 2.

THE HOLY FAMILY

The STORY of this Feast . . .

THE Boy Jesus grew up in the little town of Nazareth. Joseph was a carpenter, and the people of the town must often have seen Jesus help him in his shop. Though Jesus was a Boy like other boys, He was the Son of God. He could not sin. He loved God with all His Heart. He was always kind and wanted to help people.

When Jesus was twelve years old, He went to Jerusalem with His parents to join in the Passover Feast. After the Feast Mary and Joseph noticed that Jesus was not with them and sought Him for three days. They found him in the Temple listening to the teachers of the law and asking them questions. He said to His mother: "Did you not know that I must be busy with My Father's work?"

Jesus went back to Nazareth with Mary and Joseph and always obeyed them.

The MEANING of this Feast . . .

THE Holy Family is the model of all Christian families. It shows us how to live.

The feast of the Holy Family is celebrated the Sunday after Christmas.

THE BAPTISM OF JESUS

The STORY of this Feast . . .

GREAT crowds came out to hear John preach in the desert, near the Jordan River. Many of the people were sorry for their sins and asked to be baptized.

One day John saw Jesus Himself coming among the people to be baptized. When all the people were baptized, and Jesus was at prayer after also being baptized, the skies opened and the Holy Spirit came on Him like a dove. And a voice came from heaven: "You are My beloved Son. I am pleased with You."

The MEANING of this Feast . . .

THE Holy Spirit came upon Jesus not to make Him holy, but to anoint Him for His mission of saving the world. The voice of the heavenly Father made Jesus known as His own Son Whom He loved, and Whom He was sending to be the Messiah and King, the Savior Who was to offer Himself as a sacrifice on the Cross.

Jesus did not need to be baptized, because He was without sin as God's Son. When we are baptized we become children of God and the sin we got from Adam and Eve is washed away.

The Feast of the Baptism of Jesus is on the Sunday after January 6.

THE TRANSFIGURATION

The STORY of this Feast . . .

ONE day Jesus took with Him Peter and James and his brother John and led them up a high mountain where they could be alone. While they were up on the mountain, a change came over Jesus.

His face shone like the sun, and His clothes became as white as the light. On His face there was a heavenly majesty. Moses and Elijah came down from heaven to talk with Him.

A bright cloud covered them with its shadow, and from the cloud there came a voice which said: "This is My own dear Son, with Whom I am pleased. Listen to Him!"

The three disciples fell down with fear. But Jesus said to them: "Get up. Do not be afraid." When they raised their eyes, Jesus stood there alone.

The MEANING of this Feast . . .

WHEN Jesus was transfigured He allowed a ray of His hidden Divine glory to shine through His body.

The voice of the heavenly Father coming from the cloud told us that Jesus is His Son and our Teacher and Priest.

The Feast of the Transfiguration of Our Lord is August 6.

PALM SUNDAY

The STORY of this Feast . . .

A WHOLE crowd of men and women and children went out from Jerusalem to meet Jesus in Bethany. The disciples put some of their clothes upon the back of a colt for a saddle for Jesus to ride upon.

The large crowd spread their cloaks on the road, while some of them began to cut branches from the trees and spread them on the road.

The people were all shouting: "Hosanna to the Son of David! Blessed be He Who comes in the Name of the Lord!"

When the parade reached Jerusalem, all the people came out of their houses to see the crowd waving palm branches. "Who is this?" people asked. "This is Jesus the Prophet," replied the crowd, "the Man from Nazareth in Galilee!"

The MEANING of this Feast . . .

JESUS entered Jerusalem to show that He wanted to rule over the souls of men. He should reign as King in our own heart and life.

Palm Sunday is the beginning of Holy Week.

HOLY THURSDAY

The STORY of this Feast . . .

AS Jesus and His Apostles were eating the Last Supper, Jesus took some bread, and when He had blessed it, He broke it and gave it to them. "Take it and eat," he said; "this is My Body."

Then He took a cup, and when He had thanked His heavenly Father He gave it to them. "Drink all of you from this," He said, "for this is My Blood, the Blood of the new Covenant, which is to be poured out for many for the forgiveness of sins. Do this as a remembrance of Me."

The MEANING of this Feast . . .

FOR the first time Jesus said the words by which He changed bread and wine into His own Body and Blood. He gave His Apostles the power to do what He did, so that after them the priests would offer the Holy Sacrifice of the Mass till the end of time, and give us His Body and Blood in Holy Communion as Food for our soul.

Jesus gave us the Holy Eucharist and the Holy Priesthood on Holy Thursday night. It was the beginning of His Passion. This is the feast of the institution of the Holy Eucharist.

GOOD FRIDAY

The STORY of this Feast . . .

FROM noon on, darkness fell upon the whole land and lasted till the middle of the afternoon. For three hours Jesus was suffering from the pain of the nails in His bleeding hands and feet. He cried out: "My God, My God, why have You forsaken Me?"

His mother stood near the cross. Jesus said to His mother: "Woman, there is your son." Then He said to the disciple John: "There is your mother."

He cried out: "I am thirsty." Someone dipped a sponge into a dish of vinegar, and raised it to His mouth upon a stick.

Knowing that His work was done, Jesus cried out in a loud voice: "It is finished. Father, in Your hands I place My spirit."

And having said this, Jesus died.

The MEANING of this Feast . . .

JESUS gave His life to save us from our sins. In His great love and goodness He suffered death for us, and by this death He won life for us.

We must want to use our life to love and serve Him.

I devoutly kiss the Cross
on which You died for love of me.

EASTER SUNDAY

The STORY of this Feast . . .

AT dawn on Easter Sunday morning, all at once the earth began to tremble. The watchmen at the tomb of Jesus were afraid. A mighty angel of the Lord came down from heaven and rolled away the stone and sat upon it. The watchmen fell to the ground like dead men. Jesus rose from the dead by His own power. In His holy Resurrection our Lord's Body was glorified by being united again to His glorified Soul.

Early that morning women came to the tomb bringing spices. They entered the tomb, but did not find the body of Jesus. Two angels in white clothes stood beside them and said: "Why do you look for the Living One among the dead? He is not here; He has been raised up. Remember that He said He would be crucified, and on the third day rise again."

The MEANING of this Feast . . .

THE Resurrection was the beginning of the glorious life of Jesus. It is the strongest proof that He is the Son of God. The whole truth and meaning of our faith rests upon it. Easter is the greatest feast of our Lord.

ASCENSION THURSDAY

The STORY of this Feast . . .

MANY times after He came out of the grave, Jesus appeared to His friends. When the Apostles were upon a mountain in Galilee, where Jesus had told them to go, He appeared to them and told them what they must do when He had gone to heaven.

Jesus said to them: "All power in heaven and on earth has been given to Me. Go and make disciples of all the nations; baptize them in the Name of the Father, and of the Son and of the Holy Spirit, and teach them to obey all the commands I gave you. I am with you always; yes to the end of time."

Jesus raised His hands in blessing. As they watched, they saw Him rise from the ground till a cloud took Him from their eyes. He was taken up into heaven and took His seat at God's right hand.

The Apostles went back to Jerusalem with great joy to await the coming of the Holy Spirit.

The MEANING of this Feast . . .

JESUS ascended into heaven to remind us that one day we too will rise with Him and ascend to heaven. There we will praise the glory of our Father.

This Feast gives us hope of the great inheritance that awaits those who believe in the power of the risen Christ.

THE SACRED HEART OF JESUS

The STORY of this Feast . . .

A week after His resurrection Jesus stood among His Apostles in the upper room and said: "Peace be with you."

Turning to Thomas, Jesus said: "Put your finger here; look here are My hands. Give Me your hand; put it into My side. Doubt no longer but believe." And Thomas said: "My Lord and my God!"

Jesus said to Him: "Thomas, you believe because you can see Me. Blessed are those who have not seen, and yet have believed."

The side of Jesus was pierced by a soldier after His death, and at once blood and water came out. His heart was opened.

The MEANING of this Feast . . .

THE heart of Jesus is a symbol of His great love which led Him to die on the cross for us. His open heart reminds us that all grace comes to us from Him, and that He is always ready to receive us if we are sorry for our sins.

By honoring the Sacred Heart of Jesus we thank Him for His love for us, and give Him our love in return.

The feast of the Sacred Heart is celebrated on Friday of the second week after Pentecost.

CHRIST THE KING

The STORY of this Feast . . .

DURING the trial of Jesus, Pilate asked Jesus: "Are You the King of the Jews?"

Jesus answered: "My Kingdom does not belong to this world. If My Kingdom were of this world, My people would be fighting to save Me from being handed over to the Jews. My Kingdom is not here."

At this Pilate said to him: "So, then, You are a king?"

Jesus answered: "I am a king. The reason I was born is to teach the truth. Whoever loves the truth hears My voice."

The MEANING of this Feast . . .

JESUS gave Himself for us in His Passion that He might redeem us from sin and make us a people pleasing to God. We belong to Him because He saved us. He wants to be the King of our hearts.

We must give Him all our love and obey His commandments. In this way He will rule over us. Jesus received all power in heaven and on earth from His Father. He is the King of the universe. He is our way to God.

The feast of Christ the King is celebrated on the last Sunday of the Church Year.

TRINITY SUNDAY

The STORY of this Feast . . .

IN the Old Testament of the Bible we read about God showing Himself to us as the one true God. People learned that God was real, that He was faithful to His promises, and that people could be His friends if they put their trust in Him.

Jesus Christ has revealed to us the secrets of the Kingdom of heaven. The greatest of His teachings is the secret of God Himself. He has told us of the life of God. Jesus taught us that in the one God there are three Persons, each equal to each other. He told us the names of these three Divine Persons: Father, Son, and Holy Spirit.

The MEANING of this Feast . . .

GOD has revealed this mystery to us because He wants us to know Him as He is, to know as much about Him as we can that we might love Him more in return for His love for us.

Jesus revealed Himself as the eternal and divine Son of God. He revealed His Father and the third Divine Person, the Holy Spirit, Whom the Father and He, as the Risen Lord, sent to His Church.

God is our Father; Jesus Christ is our Lord and Savior; the Holy Spirit is our Sanctifier, Teacher and Guide. We may pray to any one of the three Divine Persons, living in our soul by grace.

Trinity Sunday is the Sunday after Pentecost.

PRAYER OF PRAISE

GLORY to God in the highest,
   and peace to His people on earth.
Lord God, heavenly King,
almighty God and Father,
   we worship You, we give You thanks,
   we praise You for Your glory.

Lord Jesus Christ, only Son of the Father,
Lord God, Lamb of God,
You take away the sin of the world:
   have mercy on us;
You are seated at the right hand of the Father:
   receive our prayer.

For You alone are the Holy One,
You alone are the Lord,
You alone are the Most High,
   Jesus Christ,
   with the Holy Spirit,
   in the glory of God the Father. Amen.